A STUDENT WORKBOOK
FOR
BHS STAGE ONE

D0892822

A STUDENT WORKBOOK
FOR
BHS STAGE ONE

MAXINE CAVE

BHSSM+T

J. A. ALLEN
London

For Basym

British Library Cataloguing-in-Publication Data.
A catalogue record for this book is available from the British Library.

ISBN 0.85131.825.8

Published in Great Britain in 2000 by
J. A. Allen
an imprint of Robert Hale Ltd
Clerkenwell House
45–47 Clerkenwell Green
London EC1R 0HT

Typesetting and production: Bill Ireson
Colour photography: Bob Langrish
Illustrations: Maggie Raynor
Cover design: Nancy Lawrence
Printed in Singapore by Kyodo Printing Co (S'pore) Pte Ltd

Contents

Introduction

This question-and-answer workbook will not guarantee that you pass your exam. But it will improve your chances of success and build on the work you have done on the way to the big day.

The questions are representative of those which a candidate may be asked during a BHS Stage One examination. Each examiner, of course, has his or her own way of phrasing a question, but the questions in this book are of the general type asked.

Some questions may appear very simple, asking the candidate to "state the obvious". Their inclusion here is intended to demonstrate that examiners are not asking candidates for complicated or in-depth answers at this level; they simply want to know that each candidate has acquired the basic knowledge and experience required at Stage One.

In the same way, the example answers to the questions have been selected to demonstrate the depth of knowledge sought by the examiner. Students may come up with answers that differ from those selected here. This does not necessarily mean that the answers the students have given are incorrect; to some of the questions, there can be more than one answer.

At the centre of the book students will find a section intended to prove that examiners are human too! Most people taking the exam are nervous on the day and may think that examiners are trying to catch them out. They are not; don't forget that all BHS examiners have taken and passed this exam at some stage in their career so they do know how you are feeling. So, read this section first if you want to know what the exam consists of, how it will be conducted, what is expected of you, and how the examiners will arrive at their decision.

Good luck on the day.

MAXINE CAVE

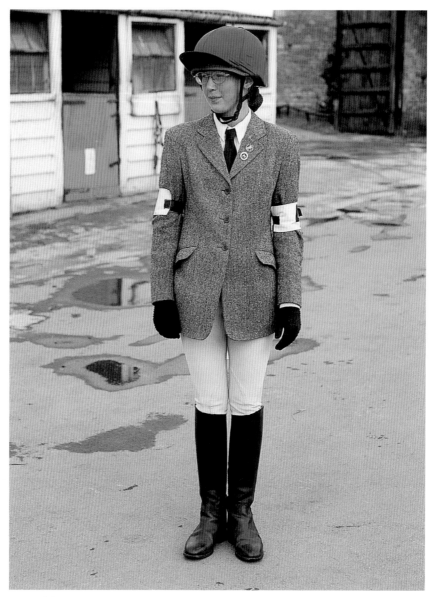

A candidate prepares to take the BHS examination

This photograph was taken under examination conditions at The Talland School of Equitation

1 Grooming

Questions

1. Why should you avoid using a plastic curry comb or dandy brush to groom the horse's mane and tail, and what are the best tools for the job?

   ....

   ....

   ....

   ....

2. How many sponges should be in the grooming kit and what are they for?

   ....

   ....

   ....

3. Which task should be performed first when grooming the horse and why?

   ....

   ....

   ....

   ....

   ....

4. Which two items of grooming kit are usually used together to clean all of the coat?

   ....

5. What is the dandy brush mainly used for?

   ....

   ....

   ....

6. Which item of grooming kit is particularly good for bringing grease and dirt to the surface of the coat, and how is it used to best effect?

   ....

   ....

7. Why should the mane be groomed before the rest of the body?

   ....

   ....

   ....

8. Why is a tail bandage sometimes used as part of the full grooming process?

   ....

   ....

   ....

This photograph was taken under examination conditions at The Talland School of Equitation

9. If the above bandage is left on too long, what could happen to the horse's tail?

    ....

    ....

    ....

10. In what circumstances would you not use a tail bandage?

....

....

11. How long should a tail bandage be left on a horse's tail?

....

12. How often should hoof oil be used?

....

....

13. What is hoof oil for?

....

14. What other products can be used on horses' hooves, and why?

....

....

15. Why do some people say that the hands are the most important grooming tools?

....

....

16. Why should gloves not be worn when grooming?

....

....

17. Apart from making the horse clean and smart, what other beneficial effects can grooming have?

....

....

....

....

18. What must you be especially careful of when grooming the horse's legs?

....

....

....

19. Why is it dangerous to kneel down when working around the horse?

....

....

....

20. Where should you stand when grooming the horse's tail?

....

....

....

....

21. On a cold day, what steps can you take to make sure a stabled horse does not become cold as you groom it?

....

....

....

22. Which brushes should you avoid using on grass-kept horses and ponies?

....

....

....

....

23. Look at the illustration on the opposite page. Name the items of grooming kit, A to K, and write your answers below.

....

....

....

....

....

....

....

....

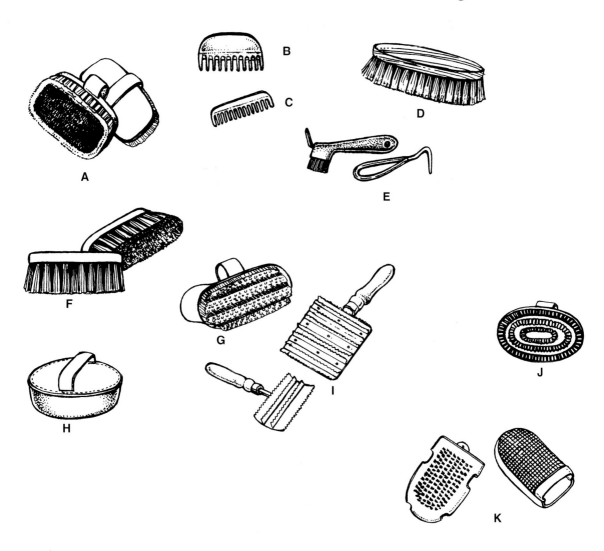

A

B

C

D

E

F

G

H

I

J

K

24. Look at the picture on the opposite page. Why should you use the body brush in your right hand when grooming the off-side of the horse?

....

....

....

....

....

25. Describe some of the new products which can help to make grooming easier.

....

....

26. When picking out the horse's feet, in which direction should you be careful to use the hoof pick and why?

....

....

....

27. If a horse is wet, why is it not a good idea to begin grooming it?

....

....

....

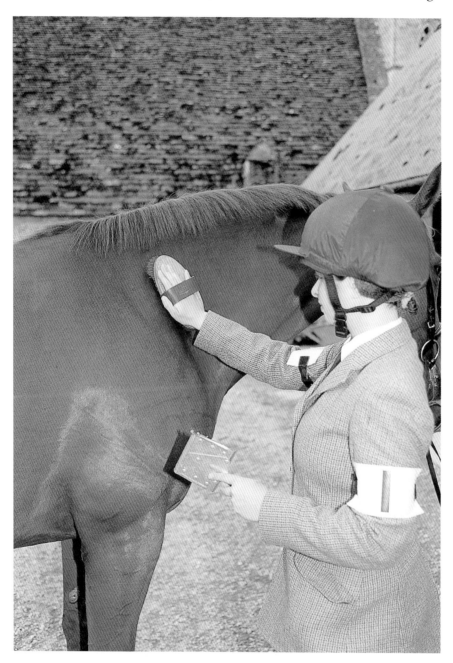

This photograph was taken under examination conditions at The Talland School of Equitation

28. What is a stable rubber and how and why is it used?

....

....

....

....

....

....

....

29. How often should the grooming kit be cleaned? Describe how you clean your own grooming kit.

....

....

....

....

....

....

....

....

....

30. When grooming the horse in its stable, why should you remove its water bucket?

    ....

    ....

    ....

31. Why should you check carefully that all items of grooming kit have been collected up and put away when you have finished?

    ....

    ....

    ....

32. Why might you consider standing on a box sometimes to groom your horse?

    ....

    ....

    ....

2 Tack and Clothing

Questions

1. When removing or putting on a rug, which has leg straps, what special care should you take?

    ....

    ....

    ....

    ....

    ....

2. Describe the procedure to follow when putting rugs on a horse.

    ....

    ....

    ....

    ....

3. Describe the procedure to follow when removing rugs from a horse.

    ....

    ....

    ....

    ....

4. What is a fillet string?

    ....

    ....

    ....

5. Describe how leg straps should be adjusted and attached.

    ....

    ....

    ....

    ....

6. What would you check, on the rug, to help you decide if it is a good fit for that horse?

    ....

    ....

    ....

    ....

7. What would you check, to make sure the rug was safe to use?

    ....

    ....

    ....

    ....

8. How would you dry and clean a wet and muddy turnout rug?

....

....

....

9. For which type of rugs are leg straps like those illustrated below used and why?

....

....

....

....

....

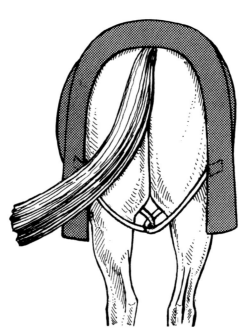

10. What injuries might a horse get from a badly-fitted rug?

    ....

    ....

    ....

11. How many turnout rugs should each horse have and why?

    ....

    ....

12. How many stable rugs should each horse have and why?

    ....

    ....

13. What are the differences between a stable rug and a turnout rug?

    ....

    ....

    ....

14. Explain what you look for and check to make sure the saddle is a comfortable fit when the horse is being ridden.

    ....

    ....

    ....

    ....

15. Look at the illustration on the opposite page. Name the parts of
the saddle, A to V, and write your answers below.

....

....

....

....

....

....

....

....

....

....

....

....

....

....

....

....

....

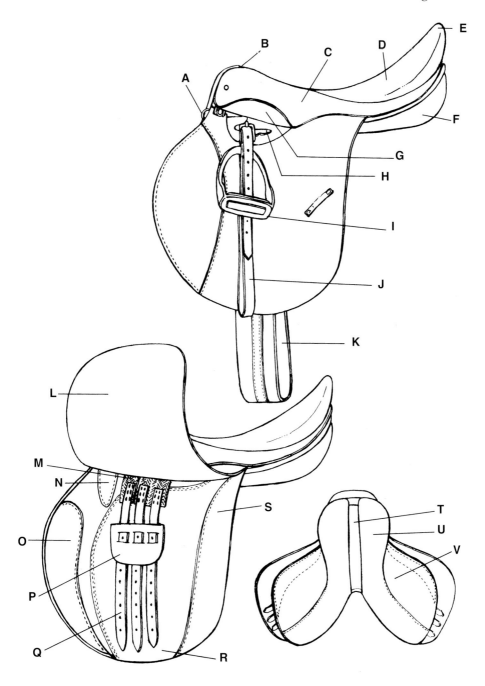

16. Which parts of a saddle should be checked for safety before it is
put on the horse?

....

....

....

....

....

17. Explain what you look for and check to make sure the bridle is
comfortable and safe for the horse.

....

....

....

....

....

18. Which parts of the bridle should be checked for safety before it is
fitted?

....

....

....

....

....

19. Look at the illustration below and name the parts of the bridle, A to G. Write your answers below.

....

....

....

....

....

....

....

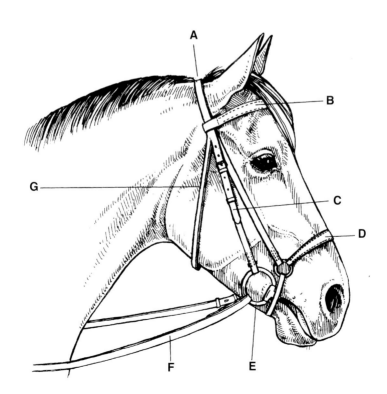

20. When you attach the girth how do you decide which of the three girth straps to use?

....

....

....

....

21. Why is one only of the three girth straps attached to a separate piece of webbing?

....

....

22. Describe how you would thoroughly clean a leather saddle and bridle.

....

....

....

....

23. Describe how you would clean a synthetic saddle and bridle.

....

....

....

....

24. The cavesson noseband pictured below is correctly positioned. What guidelines should be followed when adjusting the noseband?

....

....

....

....

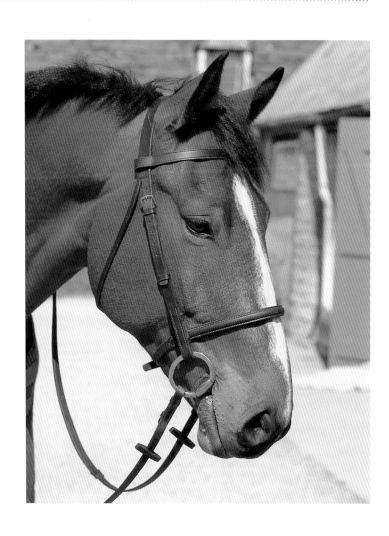

25. When you fit a saddle pad or numnah, how should it be adjusted so that it sits comfortably under the saddle?

....

....

....

....

....

26. After each use, which parts of the tack should always be cleaned?

....

....

....

....

27. What injuries to the horse may be caused if a dirty and ill-fitting saddle is used?

....

....

....

....

....

28. What injuries to the horse may be caused if a dirty and ill-fitting bridle is used?

    ....

    ....

    ....

    ....

    ....

29. Which parts of the tack are most likely to become worn and break when in use?

    ....

    ....

    ....

    ....

    ....

30. Why must special care be taken when carrying and putting down saddles?

    ....

    ....

    ....

    ....

    ....

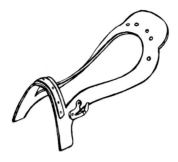

31. What is the illustration above? Explain its function.

....

....

....

....

32. Why should you always run up the stirrups on your saddle when you have dismounted and when you are leading the horse around the yard?

....

....

....

....

....

33. Why is it not a good idea to leave a saddle on the stable door while preparing the horse?

....

....

....

....

....

34. Describe how you take special care to avoid hurting the horse when putting on or taking off a saddle, and explain which parts of the horse are particularly vulnerable.

....

....

....

....

....

35. When a horse is tacked up in the stable why should it always be tied up if you have to leave it alone?

....

....

....

....

36. Look at the picture below. The throatlatch on the horse's bridle looks loose. What is the function of the throatlatch and how should it be adjusted?

....

....

....

....

....

37. Describe how you take special care to avoid hurting the horse when putting on or taking off a bridle, and explain which parts of the horse are particularly vulnerable.

....

....

....

....

....

38. If you have to leave the horse in the stable with its bridle on, how do you secure the reins, to make sure they do not slip down and get caught in the horse's legs?

....

....

....

....

....

3 Shoeing

Questions

1. Name the parts of the horse's foot, A–N, illustrated below. Write your answers on the opposite page.

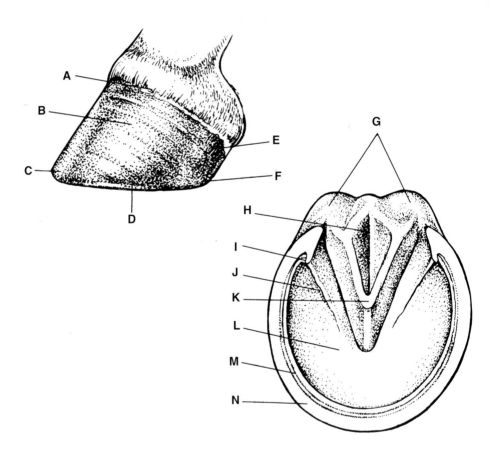

....

....

....

....

....

....

....

....

....

....

....

....

....

2. What and where are the clenches?

....

....

....

....

....

3. What is meant by "risen clenches"?

....

....

....

....

4. Give four indicators that show a horse needs to be re-shod.

....

....

....

....

....

5. Look at the picture on the opposite page. What is the farrier using to support the horse's foot?

....

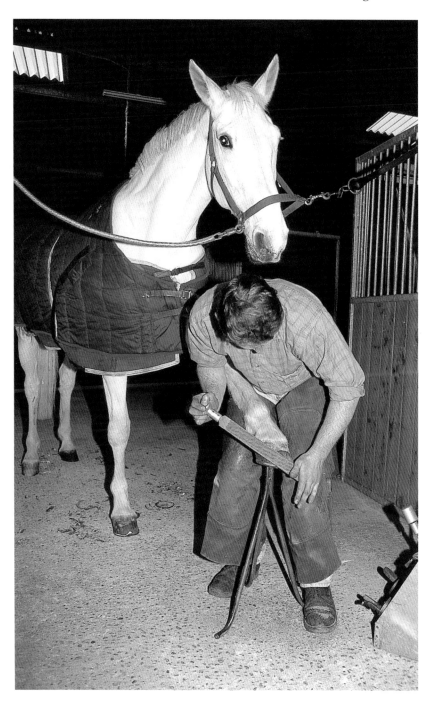

6. How often does a horse usually need to be re-shod?

....

7. What factors contribute towards the frequency with which a horse needs re-shoeing?

....

....

....

....

8. What is meant by "overgrown feet"?

....

....

9. If your horse's shoes are firmly in place and they look in good condition, but the horse's feet are long, why would you still ask the farrier to re-shoe?

....

....

10. If the horse's shoes are wearing a little thin, why is it not a good idea to go out riding on the roads?

....

....

....

4 Routine Daily Tasks

Questions

1. If asked to stand a horse up for inspection how would you try to
    make the horse stand and why?

    ....

    ....

    ....

2. If a vet has to administer treatment to your horse, would you
    hold it using a headcollar or a bridle, and why?

    ....

    ....

3. Describe how you would go about leading a horse correctly and
    safely around the yard or to and from the field.

    ....

    ....

    ....

4. Describe how you would trot up a horse in hand for someone to
    look at.

    ....

    ....

    ....

5. How does the picture above show good points for leading a horse in hand?

   ....

   ....

   ....

   ....

6. Why might you use a bridle for trotting a horse in hand?

   ....

   ....

7. Explain the importance of tying up a haynet correctly.

    ....

    ....

    ....

8. Explain the principles of the correct lifting procedures for heavy
    items.

    ....

    ....

    ....

9. In the illustration below, what is the person doing wrong?

    ....

    ....

10. When leading horses in and out of stables what particular points of care should you be aware of?

    ....

    ....

    ....

    ....

11. What items of clothing might you wear to aid your safety when leading and trotting up horses?

    ....

    ....

    ....

12. How should you stand when holding a horse for the farrier or vet?

    ....

    ....

13. How would you go about carrying buckets of water from A to B?

    ....

    ....

    ....

    ....

5 Bedding and Mucking Out

Questions

1. Name some types of bedding.

    ....

    ....

    ....

    ....

2. Which tools would you usually use for the mucking out of a straw bed?

    ....

    ....

    ....

    ....

3. Which tools would you usually use for the mucking out of a shavings bed?

    ....

    ....

    ....

    ....

4. Describe what is happening in this illustration.

....

....

....

....

5. What is meant by "deep litter"?

....

....

....

6. Outline the procedure for the full mucking out of a straw bed.

    ....

    ....

    ....

    ....

    ....

    ....

7. Why should all stable tools have a particular place in which they
    can be safely stored?

    ....

    ....

    ....

    ....

    ....

8. Outline the procedure for the full mucking out of a shavings bed.

    ....

    ....

    ....

    ....

    ....

9. Why should a horse always be tied up if it is in the stable while being mucked out?

    ....

    ....

10. What type of fork is illustrated below? And describe what the other items of stable equipment are used for.

    ....

    ....

    ....

    ....

11. Why should you remove the horse's water bucket before you begin mucking out?

    ....

    ....

    ....

12. How should you position the wheelbarrow if the horse is in the stable while you are mucking out?

    ....

    ....

    ....

    ....

13. Why is a wheelbarrow a hazard around the stable yard?

    ....

    ....

    ....

    ....

14. What is meant by "skipping up" (or "skipping out" as it is sometimes known)?

    ....

    ....

    ....

15. In this picture what type of bedding does the horse have? And what tools would you use to skip up droppings from this bed?

....

....

....

....

....

16. What type of bedding is shown in this picture? And what tools would you use to skip up droppings from this bed?

....

....

....

....

....

17. How often would you skip up your horse's stable?

....

18. Why is it a good idea to pick out a horse's feet into a skip?

....

....

19. Why is it a good idea to skip up?

....

....

20. Why is it safer to use rubber gloves rather than a stable fork when skipping up?

....

....

21. Why is a muck heap a fire hazard?

....

....

....

22. Where should a muck heap be sited, and why?

....

....

....

23. Why is it important to build a tidy muck heap, like this one?

   ....

   ....

   ....

   ....

24. Explain the importance of keeping all yard areas tidy and well
    swept.

   ....

   ....

   ....

   ....

25. What do you understand by the term "setting fair"?

   ....

6 Points of the Horse, Colours and Markings

Questions

1. Look at the illustration on the opposite page. Name the points of the horse, A to L. Write your answers below.

....

....

....

....

....

....

....

....

....

....

....

....

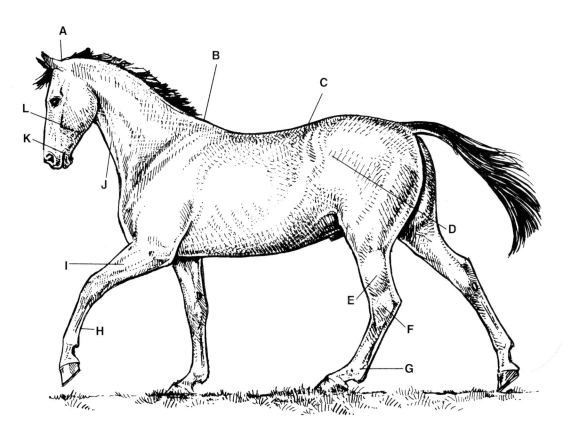

2. Look at the illustration on the opposite page. Name (*top*) the face markings A to E and (*bottom*) the leg markings F to I. Write your answers below.

....

....

....

....

....

....

....

....

....

....

....

....

....

....

....

....

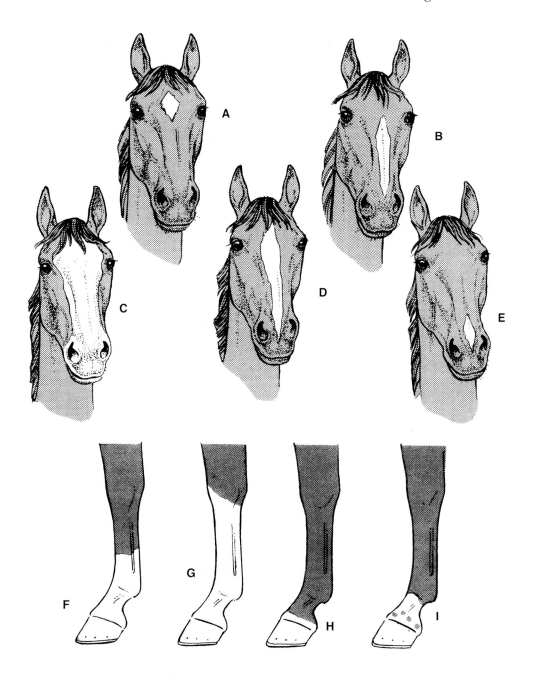

3. How many pasterns does a horse have?

....

4. What is an ergot?

....

....

5. How many chestnuts does a horse have and what are they?

....

....

....

6. Where is the horse's dock?

....

7. Why is it necessary to learn the points of the horse?

....

....

....

....

8. Describe the difference between a sock and a stocking.

....

....

9. What distinguishing features make a bay horse a bay?

....

....

....

....

10. What features make a chestnut horse chestnut?

....

....

....

....

11. What is a dorsal or eel strip?

....

....

....

....

12. What is a snip?

....

....

....

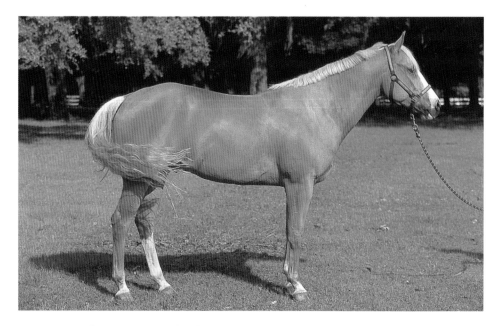

13. What colour is the horse above?

....

14. What colour is the horse below?

....

15. What colour is the horse below?

....

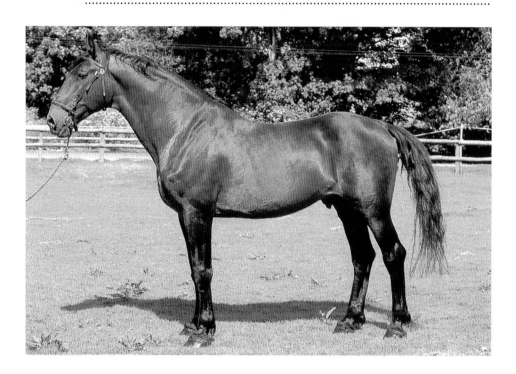

16. What is a blaze?

....

....

17. In terms of horses' markings, what is a star?

....

....

18. How is a horse with large, random, brown and white patches over its coat described?

....

....

19. How is a horse with large, random, black and white patches over its coat described?

....

....

20. In the illustration below what is the person doing and what is the item of equipment he is using?

....

....

....

....

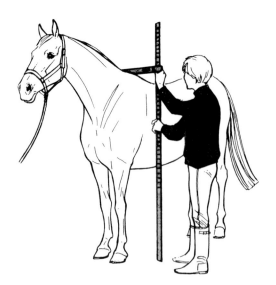

21. Name three different types of grey colouring of horses.

....

....

....

22. Name three different types of roan colouring.

....

....

....

23. What are ermine marks?

....

....

7 Horse Behaviour

Questions

1. If looking at a group of horses out in the field how would you expect to see them behaving?

   ....

   ....

   ....

   ....

   ....

2. Would you expect to see different behaviour on a wet winter day from that on a hot summer day? If so, how would it differ?

   ....

   ....

   ....

   ....

   ....

3. Describe three instincts of the horse.

   ....

   ....

   ....

4. If a horse on its own in a stable is frightened by something it cannot see making a noise, what would you expect the horse to do?

....

....

5. If a group of horses such as the one below is suddenly frightened by something what are the horses likely to do?

....

....

....

6. If you are riding out and one of the horses in your group is fright-
    ened by something, what would you expect it and the other
    horses to do?

    ....

    ....

    ....

    ....

    ....

7. What sort of objects might frighten a horse out on a ride?

    ....

    ....

    ....

    ....

    ....

8. When riding out, would you expect any problems to occur if a
    group of riders decided to separate the horses, some taking one
    route while the others followed a different route? If so, what
    would these problems be?

    ....

    ....

    ....

    ....

9. If selecting a horse for a novice rider, how important is it to take into account the horse's temperament, and why?

    ....

    ....

    ....

    ....

    ....

10. Describe the behaviour of the horses below.

    ....

    ....

11. Describe the behaviour of these horses.

....

....

12. What signs would lead you to think that a horse was feeling "fresh", and what is meant by this term?

....

....

....

13. What signs might the horse you are riding display when it is not happy with another horse coming too close?

....

....

....

....

....

14. When observing horses out in the field what behaviour might you see in one horse that may make you concerned about its health?

....

....

....

....

15. If several horses from a group are brought in from the field and just one is left behind, how might that horse behave and why?

....

....

....

....

....

16. Why is routine so important in the management of horses?

....

....

....

....

....

17. Give examples of routines you follow with your horses.

....

....

....

....

....

18. What sort of problem behaviour could cause injury among a group of horses living in the field together?

....

....

....

....

....

19. If you introduced a new horse into a field with an established group, what sort of behaviour are you likely to see?

    ....

    ....

    ....

20. When a horse has not been turned out for a long time, how is it likely to behave when released into the field?

    ....

    ....

    ....

21. What steps would you take to make sure your horse is happy and relaxed in the stable?

    ....

    ....

    ....

22. What sort of behaviour would lead you to think that a horse was not going to be easy to handle in the stable?

    ....

    ....

    ....

    ....

23. Why should you always talk to your horse when approaching it in the stable?

   ....

   ....

   ....

24. What precautions do you take when handling a horse said to be badly behaved in the stable?

   ....

   ....

   ....

25. When working around a horse in the stable why should you always touch the horse on its shoulder or neck before moving on to its hindquarters or legs?

   ....

   ....

   ....

26. Would you expect to find your horse lying down in the stable? If so, is it a good thing if it does?

   ....

   ....

   ....

   ....

27. Why is it important to follow the same routine when carrying out daily tasks with your horse?

....

....

....

....

28. What type of stabling layout is likely to make horses feel more relaxed and why?

....

....

....

....

8 The Horse's Health

Questions

1. List several points that indicate a horse is in good health.

....

....

....

....

....

....

....

2. List several points that indicate a horse is not in good health.

....

....

....

....

....

....

....

3. This horse is a picture of good health. List four points which illustrate this.

   ....

   ....

   ....

   ....

   ....

4. What can you tell about a horse's health by looking at its coat?

   ....

   ....

5. What can you tell about a horse's health by looking at its drop-pings?

   ....

   ....

   ....

   ....

   ....

6. When running your hands over a horse, what can you find out about its health?

   ....

   ....

   ....

   ....

7. What might your horse's behaviour tell you about its state of health?

   ....

   ....

   ....

8. What is meant by a "staring coat"?

    ....

    ....

9. Why is it particularly important to make a special check on your horse last thing at night and first thing in the morning?

    ....

    ....

    ....

    ....

10. What would you look for when checking your horse last thing at night?

    ....

    ....

    ....

    ....

11. What would you look for when checking your horse first thing in the morning?

    ....

    ....

    ....

    ....

12. How does the type of stabling pictured above help to keep horses relaxed and happy?

....

....

....

....

....

....

13. Why is it so important to inform the stable manager immediately if you have even the smallest worry about the health of any of the horses in your care?

....

....

....

14. What might you observe about your horse that would make you call the vet?

....

....

....

....

9 Care of the Horse and the Horse's Field

Questions

1. What should you check for in the horse's field every day?

   ....

   ....

   ....

   ....

   ....

2. Why is it so important to make these daily checks?

   ....

   ....

   ....

   ....

3. What should you make sure the horse is provided with in the field?

   ....

   ....

   ....

4. What measures can you take on a daily basis to help keep the field in good condition?

....

....

....

5. What are the hazards of using fencing of the type illustrated below?

....

....

....

....

6. Describe other measures you can take to help keep a field in good condition for grazing horses.

....

....

....

....

....

....

7. What is meant by a "horse sick" field?

....

....

....

....

....

8. If a field becomes horse sick, what measures can be taken to return it to good condition?

....

....

....

9. Describe the steps you should take when turning one or more horses out into the field.

....

....

....

....

....

....

10. How would you go about catching a well-behaved horse in the field?

....

....

....

....

11. How would you go about catching a horse which does not want to be caught?

....

....

....

....

....

12. What procedure would you follow when bringing one or more horses out of the field?

....

....

....

....

13. Why is it not a good idea to take a bucket of feed into the field when there are several horses there together?

....

....

14. When horses are living out and wearing turnout rugs, what extra checks must you make every day?

....

....

....

15. What special checks should you make when horses are living out during summer weather?

....

....

....

....

16. List and describe three good points about this type of fencing.

    ....

    ....

    ....

    ....

17. What conditions in the field may cause health problems for your horse during the winter?

    ....

    ....

    ....

18. Why is the water trough pictured above a good arrangement?

....

....

....

....

10 Feeding and Watering

Questions

1. List the main rules of feeding, and give reasons for each rule.

....

....

....

....

....

....

....

....

....

....

....

....

....

....

....

2. List the main rules of watering, and give reasons for each rule.

....

....

....

....

....

....

....

....

....

3. What would you look for to see if a sample of horse and pony nuts is a good sample?

....

....

....

4. What would lead you to the conclusion that the horse and pony nuts are of inferior quality?

....

....

5. In a sample of rolled oats like the one above, what would you look for to see if it is of good quality?

....

....

....

....

6. What would lead you to the conclusion that a sample of rolled oats is of inferior quality?

....

....

....

....

7. What would you look for to see if a sample of shredded sugar beet is of good quality?

....

....

....

....

....

8. What would lead you to the conclusion that the shredded sugar beet is of inferior quality?

....

....

....

....

....

9. What would you look for to see if a sample of coarse mix is of good quality?

....

....

....

....

....

10. What would lead you to the conclusion that the coarse mix is of poor quality?

....

....

....

....

11. In a sample of bran like the one below, what would you look for to see if it is of good quality?

....

....

....

12. What would lead you to the conclusion that the bran is of poor quality?

....

....

....

....

....

13. How do you tell the difference between oats and barley?

....

....

....

....

....

14. What would you look for to see if a sample of molassed chaff is of good quality?

....

....

....

....

....

15. What would lead you to the conclusion that the molassed chaff is of inferior quality?

....

....

....

....

....

16. What would you look for to see if a sample of meadow hay is of good quality?

....

....

....

....

....

17. What would lead you to the conclusion that the meadow hay is of poor quality?

....

....

....

....

18. If you fed poor quality feed or hay to your horse what effect could it have on the horse's health?

....

....

....

....

....

19. What is meant by "hard" or "concentrate" feed?

....

....

....

....

....

20. What type of hard feed might you give to a 14.2 hh pony, in light work and stabled during the winter?

....

....

....

....

....

21. How much hard feed would you give to this 14.2 hh pony and how would you divide it during the day?

....

....

....

....

....

22. How much hay would you give to this pony, and what factors would help you to decide how much to give?

....

....

....

....

....

....

23. What type of hard feed might you give to this same pony if it was in light work and kept out at grass all winter?

....

....

....

....

24. How much hard feed would you give to this pony?

....

....

....

....

25. How much hay would you give to this pony?

....

....

....

....

26. What type of hard feed would you give to a 15.3 hh horse in light work, and stabled throughout the winter?

....

....

....

....

27. How much hard feed would you give to this horse?

....

....

....

28. How much hay would you give to this horse?

....

....

....

....

29. What type of hard feed would you give to this horse if it was living out at grass all winter?

....

....

....

....

30. How much hard feed would you give to this horse in these circumstances?

....

....

....

31. How much hay would you give to this horse in these circumstances?

....

....

....

11 General Knowledge

Questions

1. When riding out on the road, what extra clothing and equipment will help make you and your horse more visible to drivers?

    ....

    ....

    ....

    ....

    ....

2. Should you walk and trot horses along verges, or stay on the road?

    ....

    ....

    ....

3. If a group of riders need to cross the road should they cross one or two at a time, so as not to hold up drivers and to allow vehicles through?

    ....

    ....

    ....

    ....

4. What could you add to this horse's tack to help with safety when riding out on the road?

....

....

....

....

....

....

This photograph was taken under examination conditions at The Talland School of Equitation

5. Why is it a good idea to use knee boots, as pictured above, when riding on the road?

....

....

....

....

6. Apart from the traffic, what should you look out for as you ride along the road?

....

....

....

....

7. Should you trot on the road?

....

....

....

8. If you are leading a horse along the road, what equipment do you need?

....

....

....

....

9. When leading along the road, what side of the road should you keep to?

....

....

....

10. Name four points of country lore you should observe when riding out in the countryside?

....

....

....

....

....

....

....

....

11. Before going out for a ride, for the sake of safety, what should you tell another person?

....

....

....

12. If you meet other riders or pedestrians when out on a ride what is the safest and most courteous way to approach them?

....

....

....

13. Is it always a good idea to keep to single file when riding on the roads?

    ....

    ....

    ....

14. Why is it important to make sure your horse is well schooled if you are going to ride out on the roads?

    ....

    ....

    ....

15. What would you do if you are out on the roads and one of your ride falls off their horse and (a) the horse runs loose and (b) the rider is still on the ground, conscious but hurt?

    ....

    ....

    ....

    ....

    ....

    ....

    ....

    ....

16. If a rider falls off and is unconscious, what would you do?

....

....

....

....

....

....

....

....

....

17. If you are riding out and one of your ride falls off and hits their head, would you advise them to remount if they want to?

....

....

....

....

18. All yards should have a "FIRE" notice. What should be printed on the notice?

....

....

19. What precautions can you take to help prevent fire in the yard?

....

....

....

....

20. What items should be to hand in the event of a fire breaking out?

....

....

....

....

....

21. Describe four aims of the British Horse Society.

....

....

....

....

....

After the BHS exam. Candidates take a well-earned break

This photograph was taken under examination conditions at The Talland School of Equitation

Exam Notes

Apply to the examinations office of the British Horse Society for application forms, a syllabus and the current fees.

Examiners are human

1. *The jobs they have*

- The majority of examiners work within the horse industry; for example, full- or part-time at agricultural colleges as lecturers in equine studies, or maybe as a yard manager for the equine department at the college.
- Some examiners have their own equine businesses, which may involve livery, schooling, competing, and/or teaching.
- Other examiners may no longer work in the equine industry, but generally have maintained links with the horse world by owning their own horses and competing in their spare time.
- By means of such jobs and connections, examiners keep up-to-date and are aware of new trends and new ways considered acceptable for carrying out certain tasks. Therefore, candidates should not think that examiners are out of date, or out of touch with current trends.

2. *Examiners go through the exam system too*

- All examiners will have worked their way through the same examination system as that which candidates themselves are working through.
- Older examiners may well have qualified before more recent changes to the BHS examination system; nonetheless, they still have had to take the BHS examination to qualify.
- Having been through the exam system themselves (some of them very recently), examiners are well aware of how stressful exams can be and know what candidates are going through.
- Individual candidates may have to go through the process of

having to re-take an examination. Likewise, some examiners themselves may have been unsuccessful and therefore will have gone through this experience too.

3. *Examiner training*

- All examiners have to attend regular examiner training days to be eligible to continue as an examiner.
- These training days take different forms. At regional level, for example, examiners often take turns in role play. Here, one examiner is the candidate and one is the examiner and another is an observer. In this way, each examiner can experience the taking of an examination from each different person's point of view.
- National examiner training days often take the form of lecture demonstrations and question and answer sessions. This gives examiners a chance to share ideas and learn new techniques.
- Examiner training puts examiners in a similar position to candidates. They experience being asked questions and have to carry out tasks under scrutiny.
- So, candidates should understand that examiners really do know how those being tested are feeling on the day, as they will have been through a similar situation, quite recently, themselves.
- Examiners also have to hold a current First Aid certificate to meet health and safety requirements. The certificate only lasts for three years at a time. Thereafter, examiners must attend a refresher course and sit the First Aid examination every three years.
- Once again, examiners experience first hand the exam situation as a candidate themselves. So they know how you are feeling.

4. *They want to pass you*

- There is nothing more pleasant for examiners than being able to pass all the candidates at an exam day.
- For examiners, the day passes quickly and easily if the candidates are well prepared and up to standard.
- It is hard work trying to gain information from a candidate who is struggling with the tasks and questions.
- Examiners will "feel" the stress of a candidate who is not coping

and this makes for an uncomfortable and sometimes worrying exam session.

- Candidates who are unsuccessful are given brief written reports, which outline where they made mistakes in the exam. This is all more work for examiners and makes for a long day.
- There is nothing better than a day when everyone passes.

5. *The role of the Chief Examiner*

- The Chief Examiner is an experienced examiner whose task it is to oversee the entire exam day. He or she will endeavour to see a small piece of work in every section of the exam, in order to gain an overview of the abilities of each candidate.
- Before the exam day, the Chief Examiner will have received a list of candidates and a list of the examiners who will make up the examining team for the day.
- The Chief Examiner will contact each member of the exam team, and let them know which section of the exam they are to examine. In this way each examiner can be prepared for their section.
- The Chief Examiner will also contact the examination centre and discuss the plan for the day and agree on the format to follow.
- On the day, the Chief Examiner will meet up with the examining team and make sure everyone is prepared. He or she will then introduce themselves and the examining team to the candidates and make sure that all those taking the exam have arrived.
- A number is allocated to each candidate. This helps the exam team identify each candidate without mistakes. At this stage, also, candidates are provided with a programme for the day so that they all know where they are supposed to be and when.
- Throughout the day the Chief Examiner will "float", moving from one section to another, keeping an eye on the time, and prompting examiners to bring their section to a conclusion if necessary.
- The Chief Examiner will endeavour to take down results from each examiner as each section is completed, in order to keep track of the day's progress.

- At the end of the day, the Chief Examiner compiles results with the aid of the exam team, and fills in the official results sheet which will be returned to the examinations office.
- From 1 January 2002 candidates' results will be posted to them.
- Candidates will be required to supply a stamped addressed envelope for this purpose, when applying to take the exam.
- Finally, the Chief Examiner will debrief any of the examiners as he or she thinks necessary and then say a thank you for the day to the host at the examination centre before leaving. On return home, or as soon as possible, the Chief Examiner posts examination results and copies of any report forms that were filled in to the examinations office of the BHS where the official results are recorded.

6. *Candidate preparation*

- When taking the first three stages of the BHS examinations, candidates can take the exams at the same centre at which they have trained. Some candidates will train at a centre, then take the exam elsewhere. There can be advantages and disadvantages to both.
- Training, then taking the exam at the same centre helps the candidate to feel "at home" and relaxed. He or she will know their way around, and know the horses they are working with. They will be familiar with the yard staff and able to ask for help easily, and will usually have their equipment to hand. For example, it is unlikely that they will find they have left their hat or boots at home.
- However, it is easy to be "sloppy" when working in familiar surroundings and with familiar horses. This can lead to mistakes and make a poor impression.
- Candidates taking the exam at an unfamiliar centre are more likely to be on their best behaviour, treating all horses with caution and being more particular about tasks when using unfamiliar equipment.

- However, they have the disadvantage of not knowing their way around and may find it more difficult to relax amongst people they do not know.
- It is essential that all candidates read the exam syllabus. When taking the exam, you must feel confident, in your own mind, that you have covered every single item on the syllabus and that you fully understand it.
- Each individual must be responsible for their own training. Too many candidates rely totally on their trainers to make sure they have covered all the necessary subjects. If you missed a lecture, one day, for whatever reason, it is not up to the trainer to make sure you cover the missed subject. It is up to you. You must take responsibility for your own training.
- Take great care to make sure that you have the correct clothing and equipment for the day. It is quite a good idea to have a dress rehearsal. If you try out your intended exam clothing, you can check that you will be comfortable riding or working in it, and you can ask an experienced person for their opinion on how you look.
- The fit and cut of a hacking jacket can make a big difference to the way you look on a horse. Your choice of working clothing can make a big difference to your performance and comfort and the impression you make.
- Always check details regarding certificates and documents that you may need to have with you on exam day. Sometimes, for example, it is necessary to show a Riding and Road Safety Certificate; you may not be allowed to complete the exam if you don't have it with you. So, check these details well in advance.
- If you are going to an unfamiliar centre to take the exam, make sure that you visit it in advance. By doing this you can check the route and how long it takes to get there. On arrival, introduce yourself and ask if you can have a look round. Most centres are always happy to show you around so that you can familiarise yourself with the layout. In this way you will feel more confident on the day.

- Sometimes it is helpful to have a doctor's note if you have a condition that examiners should know about. For example, if you are asthmatic and need an inhaler, examiners would rather know about it, then they can allow you to use your inhaler as necessary.
- However, it is not a good idea to bring a doctor's certificate which says that you have a hip/leg/arm, etc., injury. Whilst examiners will take into consideration problems like ongoing chronic conditions, if you are not fit to take the exam, you should not be there at all.

7. Coping with the day

- Always plan to arrive early. This will give you time to find your way around the centre. For example, you need to locate the reception area, and the toilets.
- If you are taking a riding exam, the jumping course will be laid out ready, and candidates are encouraged to walk the course at the start of the day.
- Some centres have refreshment facilities, or you may bring refreshments with you. Take time to sit and relax and have something to drink while you compose yourself.
- It is always a good idea to have someone accompany you to the exam. Having someone to talk to, who can also take care of your belongings during the day, and perhaps be ready with a change of coat, etc., as necessary, is reassuring specially at an unfamiliar centre.
- Another good idea is to have someone drive you to and from the exam. A candidate who is nervous with anticipation of the exam day, and then afterwards may be tired, elated, or disappointed, is not in the best frame of mind to concentrate on driving.
- Make sure you take all the equipment you will need. For example, hat, boots, gloves, hairnet, jacket, pens, any certificates required, are all easily forgotten. Take different coats for changing weather and any other spare items you may like to have with you just in case.
- Be friendly towards the other candidates. You may find it reassuring to find that they are just as nervous as you are, but don't

let another candidate make you feel more nervous. Occasionally you may come across a candidate who feels the need to show off how much knowledge and experience they have. This may leave you feeling inadequately prepared, if you take too much notice. However, you will probably discover that they know no more than you do; they just feel the need to show off as it makes them feel more confident, when underneath they are really very nervous.

- During the course of the day, you will be examined in groups of four or five – or maybe more, depending upon the total number of candidates. At Stage One, there can be up to 18 candidates taking the exam.
- Each group session will last threequarters of an hour to one hour.
- The Stage One exam is completed in one morning, starting at 9.00 a.m. and finishing at 12.30 p.m. approximately. There will be four group sessions: Riding, Practical, Practical/Oral, and Theory.
- There are no written papers at Stage One. All question and answer sessions are verbal or practical demonstration.
- Make sure you have made arrangements for lunch. It is best to bring sandwiches with you, as this is quick and easy. Going to a local pub can take too much time, and you may find yourself missing out because you don't manage to get served on time. Lunch breaks are usually short, and examiners do not expect to wait for anyone.
- After a long car journey, and especially on a cold day, you may find yourself quite stiff, and likely to be a little rigid. If you are scheduled to ride first thing, try some loosening up exercises before you start – perhaps a quick run around the indoor school!
- It is important that you take the day seriously. However, this doesn't mean going around with a grim expression on your face. Try to keep smiling, and keep up a professional and friendly approach. Most people have a favourable impression of someone who presents themselves in this way.
- Most important of all, is not to take the exam before you are ready. You really need to be above standard to allow for nerves making you perform below your normal level on the day. If you

are only just up to standard, then on the day you are bound to fall below standard. So, don't try to rush your exams; be patient, and avoid disappointment.

8. *Examiner's expectations and what they would like to see*

- Examiners are well aware that candidates are likely to be nervous, especially at the beginning of the day. They hope that candidates will gradually settle and gain confidence as the day progresses. They will make allowances for nerves; for example, it is quite likely that some candidates will become flustered, or go to do something one way and then change their mind. Examiners will put this down to nerves and will not think badly of candidates if this happens. So, don't let your nervous feelings worry you too much.
- As candidates progress through the levels in their training, examiners will expect them to appear more confident at the corresponding exams. Examiners will, however, still allow for a degree of nervousness at the beginning of any examination.
- One of the best ways for a candidate to make a good impression, is to be enthusiastic. Candidates who stand around looking bored will not do themselves any favours. Candidates should show a keenness to carry out tasks and answer questions.
- It is important that candidates do remember that these exams are intended for professionals. Each exam stage leads towards qualifications that can result in the candidate becoming an instructor or manager in charge. It is therefore advantageous to project yourself as a mature person. For example, when talking about daily grazing management, DON'T say "poos" and DO say "droppings" need to be picked up. Think before you speak and project your mature approach by using the correct terminology.
- Throughout the day, you need to relate to the examiners and the other candidates in a positive and friendly way. Treat examiners with respect. Whether you know them or not, you should not be on Christian name terms during the exam. Give them space to make notes and to discuss points with their fellow examiners in private. At the same time, be friendly and willing to talk to them should they invite you to make conversation.

- Try to be helpful to other candidates. Don't butt in when they are trying to answer a question, but do help out – if they are struggling to find a hoof pick for example. Try not to disagree with other people; this can be unnerving for the person you disagree with. Just state your opinion. For example, you may say "I would do it this way."
- Throughout the exam, the examiners will need to spread their time amongst the candidates. When another candidate is being asked a question, or asked to perform a particular task, continue to remain aware and involved.
- For example, if a candidate is asked to trot up a horse, watch and listen. Show that you are interested. Examiners will be watching you all the time and not just when you are asked to do something specific. How you behave throughout the day will help to create an impression on the examiners.
- If the examiner says you have completed a section and that you can go on to the next, remember your training. The examiner will notice the candidate who checks that equipment has been put away tidily, that the stable door is properly bolted, and that the horse has been left secure and comfortable in its stable. So, you must be thinking all the time; it is tiring, but you are under scrutiny all through the day.
- Examiners know that mistakes are made. They do not expect candidates to go through the whole day without a single mistake. So don't panic if you think you have done something wrong. Approach the examiner and tell him or her what it is you are concerned about, and how you would like to put it right.

9. *Exam technique*

- The exam day will be tiring, but it is very important to remain alert throughout. Be aware of what is going on around you. Listen to others, and keep track of what is happening so that you can contribute at the right time. For example, another candidate may be loading a horse into a horse box, and perhaps the partition may swing loose. If you are alert you will be able to step forward and help – showing that you are aware and able when needed.

- Be tactful towards other candidates. If you think another person has answered a question incorrectly, rather than saying you disagree, or that they are wrong, simply say, for example, "I would do it this way, ..." or "In my opinion, . . . "
- Try to put yourself forward whenever there is an opportunity to do so – but not too often. If you keep on coming forward with answers, examiners will tend to give others a chance. Whereas, if you always wait to be asked for an answer, examiners will tend to keep asking you questions to find out what you know. So be forward, without being pushy.
- Make sure you use the correct technical terms whenever appropriate. This gives a professional and knowledgeable impression.
- During the day you will give a good impression if you move quickly from one place to another. As candidates finish one section, and move on to another part of the stable yard, they should aim to do so as quickly as possible. If you need a drink or a toilet break, then let the examiner know, so they're not searching for you.
- Do ask questions when necessary. If an examiner asks you to do something, or phrases a question in such a way that you don't understand what is wanted, don't be afraid to ask for clarification. All examiners know that sometimes they may be misunderstood, and are experienced in rephrasing themselves to aid understanding. Whatever you do, don't try to carry on without being completely clear about the task or question.
- Follow these guidelines and you should sail through! Good luck.

10. End of day discussions

- When the examination is over, the examiners will gather together and compare notes and compile results.
- If any reports need to be written, this will be done now.
- Each examiner will give his or her final results to the Chief Examiner. He or she will then check that all is accounted for and all paperwork has been completed.
- At this point certificates are filled in for successful candidates, and all the paperwork is completed. This can take some time.

- If there has been an accident during the day, an accident report must be filled in with all the relevant information.
- If a candidate is considered to be borderline in any part of the exam, examiners will discuss the candidate's performance and try to come to a conclusion on whether or not he or she is to be given a pass or be deemed unsuccessful. Every effort is made to highlight the candidate's positive points to see if they outweigh the negative. These discussions can take some time, and examiners will never hurry their results.
- The examiners may remain at the exam centre for some time in order to complete this paperwork. The candidates will be free to leave as soon as they have completed the exam.

Answers to the Questions

Chapter 1: **Grooming**

1. Plastic curry combs tend to break the hairs of the mane and tail, leaving them thin and untidy. The soft body brush and your fingers are the best tools to remove tangles from the mane and tail without causing damage.
2. There should be at least three sponges in each grooming kit. One sponge for cleaning the horse's eyes, one for cleaning the nostrils and muzzle, and one for cleaning under the tail.
3. It is a good idea to pick out the horse's feet as the first grooming task. This tends to be a dirty job, so by doing it first it saves making an already clean and groomed horse dirty again. As you also check the horse's shoes when doing this task, you can make sure the horse is well shod for riding and that it has not lost any shoes.
4. The body brush and metal curry comb can be used together effectively to groom the whole horse.
5. The dandy brush is a stiff bristled brush used mainly on grass-kept horses and ponies to remove mud and dried sweat from the coat, especially in winter when the coat is thick and long.
6. The rubber curry comb is an excellent tool for removing grease from the coat. The person grooming should use it vigorously in a series of small circles all over the coat. This has the effect of bringing the grease to the surface so that it can then be brushed clear of the coat with the body brush.
7. When you groom the mane, dirt and grease will fall out of it, over the horse's neck, so it would be pointless to groom other parts of the body first, then make them dirty again when you go on to groom the mane. So grooming the mane first is sensible and labour saving.
8. Horses that have fine or pulled tails may have a tail bandage put on to improve the appearance of the tail. The tail bandage makes the top section of the tail lie smooth and tidy creating a neat appearance.
9. If a tail bandage is left on for too long it can cut off the circulation

to the tail and may cause all the hair to fall out.

10. Horses that have thick full tails do not need their tails bandaged. If the owner wants to present their horse with the natural look, a tail bandage is not appropriate.

11. If a tail bandage is used, it should not be left on for more than an hour.

12. It is best not to use hoof oil too frequently as it may upset the natural balance of oils within the hoof. It is best to use it just on special occasions.

13. Hoof oil is used to make a horse look extra smart.

14. There are other products available in the form of thick ointments which can be applied to the hooves to help stimulate better growth, or to make dry cracked hooves more supple.

15. When grooming, you should constantly run your hands over the horse's coat, feeling for hidden dirt, lumps, bumps and areas of heat or sensitivity. Through feel you can discover things that would otherwise go unnoticed. So your hands are an essential grooming tool, helping you to discover potential problems before they become real problems.

16. If you wear gloves for grooming you cannot feel for these potential problems effectively. So, gloves are a barrier to effective grooming.

17. When grooming you can build a close relationship with your horse and learn a great deal about its likes and dislikes. You will find out about its character. The grooming process itself helps to massage and stimulate the horse, improving circulation and well-being. This in turn helps to promote good health.

18. The horse's legs have very little muscle covering, being mainly bones, tendons and ligaments. Therefore, it is important to take care not to knock and bruise the bony structures with the hard backs of the brushes.

19. When kneeling down it is difficult to get up and move away quickly, so it is not a good idea to kneel down near a horse. Horses can move quickly and could easily knock you over or tread on you, unintentionally, if frightened or surprised.

20. When grooming the tail stand just to one side of the horse's hindquarters. Never stand directly behind in case the horse should kick out.

21. If a horse is wearing a rug in the stable, undo the fastenings of the rug but do not remove it completely. Fold back sections of the rug so the horse always has something to keep it warm.

22. Grass-kept horses and ponies need to keep a degree of natural grease in their coats to help protect them from wet and cold. For this reason do not use brushes like the body brush and rubber curry comb as they both remove grease very efficiently. Keep to the dandy brush and plastic curry comb.

23. A. Body brush. B. Mane and tail comb. C. Mane pulling comb. D. Water brush. E. Hoof pick. F. Dandy brush. G. Plastic curry comb. H. Leather wisp or massage pad. I. Metal curry comb. J. Rubber curry comb. K. Grooming mitt.

24. When grooming the off-side of the horse, you should use the body brush in your right hand. In that way you can put the weight of your body behind the brush, therefore using it more effectively.

25. Some grooming products now on the market are available in spray dispensers. They can be applied to the coat to repel dirt and make it easier to remove. There are also sprays that can be applied to the mane and tail which help to keep them tangle free, in the same way that human hair conditioner makes hair easier to comb out.

26. Always use the hoof pick from the heel towards the toe to make sure that you do not accidentally push the hoof pick into the horse's heels or other part of its legs, so causing an injury.

27. Grooming brushes do not remove dirt from a wet coat. If you try to groom a wet horse you will just groom the dirt further into the coat and make your task more difficult. Always let the horse's coat dry out before grooming.

28. A stable rubber is a piece of cotton cloth resembling a tea towel. It is used rather like a duster. When the grooming process has been completed, you can work over the whole horse – face, body, and legs – wiping off any dust which may have settled back on the surface of the coat.

29. The grooming kit should be cleaned as soon as it gets dirty. In practical terms it should probably be done once a week. To clean the grooming kit, first remove any hair and obvious dirt from the brushes. Next, use a bowl of warm soapy water (washing-up

liquid works well) to put all the brushes into. Give them a good scrubbing, and then rinse them in clean water. Put them all somewhere clean and dry to dry out. Rubber and metal items can be washed in the same way and then dried with an old towel.

30. When you groom your horse you will disturb a certain amount of dust and dirt, some of which will inevitably settle on to the horse's water. To prevent the water from becoming dirty, remove the bucket from the stable then replace it when the grooming process is complete.

31. It is easy to mislay items of grooming kit in the horse's bedding. Any grooming items could cause injury to the horse. Check and collect up all items of kit to prevent injury and to help maintain the kit in good condition.

32. If you have to stretch up to see the top of the horse's back and hindquarters when grooming your horse, it is a good idea to stand on a box. This will enable you both to groom these areas thoroughly and see if the horse is clean and free from injury or disease.

Chapter 2: **Tack and Clothing**

1. If the leg straps on the rug swing around, they can cause injury to the horse. Before removing or putting on the rug, ensure that the leg straps are clipped up securely.

2. When putting on rugs you should avoid throwing them over the horse, which could cause injury and fright. Fold the rug in half, into a manageable size, then place it over the horse's back. Then unfold the rug carefully, making sure that the horse's coat is smoothed down in its direction of growth.

3. When removing rugs, undo all fastenings and clip, or tie up, long straps. Fold the front of the rug back, and then slide the whole rug back and over the hindquarters.

4. A fillet string is a piece of cord attached to the two back corners of a rug. It lies under the horse's tail, just below its first thigh, and is there to prevent the rear corners of the rug from blowing up in the wind.

5. Each hind leg strap should be passed between the horse's hind legs and clipped on the ring at the rear corner of the rug. The two

straps should be linked together, by passing the second strap through the first one. They should be adjusted to lie loosely around the horse's legs, approximately level with the bottom of the first thigh.

6. The rug should lie snugly around the base of the horse's neck, without appearing to be tight. It should not hang low on the horse's chest. In length, it should extend from the withers to the top of the tail, being neither too short or too long. In depth, the rug should hang down to just below the horse's belly.

7. All rug fastenings should be checked to make sure that they are not broken and that they are working correctly. All straps must be adjusted to fit the horse, and the rug should be a good fit.

8. A wet rug should be hung on a gate or door, under cover, to dry. Once dry it can be brushed clean with a stiff brush, both inside and out.

9. Leg straps are usually fitted to turnout rugs. They help to keep the rug in place while the horse is more active in the field.

10. Badly-fitted rugs can rub the horse's shoulders, its withers, and sometimes its hind legs.

11. It is a good idea to have two turnout rugs for each horse. If one rug is broken, it may take some time to repair. While one rug is being repaired, the other rug can be used. The same applies if a rug gets particularly wet. It is better for the horse if you can give it a clean, dry rug and leave the wet one to dry out in a suitable place.

12. You may need a variety of stable rugs for each horse. Different thicknesses are needed for different weather. It is also a good idea to have spares so that you can take a rug for cleaning when necessary.

13. Stable rugs do not need to be waterproof and do not need as many fastenings to secure them. Turnout rugs must be waterproof and need extra secure fastenings to help keep the rug in place, as a horse is generally more active in the field.

14. The saddle must have clear space along the length of the gullet, so that none of the rider's weight is taken on the horse's spine. This space should be checked again, once the rider is mounted. The saddle should be level on the horse's back, neither tipping up or down at the front or back. The width of the tree should be

checked to make sure it is not pinching over the withers. The saddle should not sit too far forward, where it will restrict the movement of the shoulders, and it should not extend too far back as there should not be any weight taken on the loins.

15. A. D-ring. B. Pommel. C. Waist. D. Seat. E. Cantle. F. Lining. G. Skirt. H. Stirrup bar. I. Stirrup. J. Stirrup leather. K. Girth. L. Saddle flap. M. Webbing. N. Point pocket. O. Knee roll. P. Buckle guard. Q. Girth straps. R. Panel. S. Thigh roll. T. Gullet. U. Lining. V. Panel.

16. Always check the stirrup leathers to make sure the stitching is secure. Check the girth straps to make sure they are strong and securely stitched. Check the girth is in good condition and not likely to break.

17. On the bridle, check that the browband is not tight and causing pinching behind the horse's ears. Make sure the cheek pieces are correctly adjusted so that the bit sits snugly in the corners of the horse's mouth. If a noseband is worn, make sure it is not in a position to rub any part of the horse's face. Check that the reins will be neither too long nor too short. Make sure all the stitching is in good order and that the leather is strong and not badly worn.

18. Make sure the reins are strong and that all buckles are secure and not likely to break.

19. A. Headpiece. B. Browband. C. Cheek piece. D. Drop noseband. E. Bit. F. Reins. G. Throatlatch.

20. Two of the girth straps are attached to one piece of webbing, and the other strap is attached to another piece of webbing. Always attach the girth to two straps which are on separate pieces of webbing. Then take the horse's conformation into consideration to see if using a front and back girth strap or the two front straps will help the girth to lie in the most comfortable position for that horse.

21. Each saddle has girth straps attached to two separate pieces of webbing for safety reasons. If one piece of webbing should break, the other piece of webbing will keep the girth secure. It is very unlikely that both pieces of webbing would break at the same time.

22. To thoroughly clean a leather saddle and bridle, first completely

dismantle every piece of the tack. With a damp sponge work over each piece of leather until all the grease and dirt have been removed. Take a clean damp sponge and some saddle soap then use the sponge to apply the saddle soap to the leather. Work in a generous layer of saddle soap without leaving the tack damp or sticky. Then reassemble the tack, making sure you have washed stirrup irons, bits, and any numnah or saddle pad used.

23. A synthetic saddle and bridle can be cleaned with a firm brush and some warm soapy water. Dismantle the tack first then scrub it clean, trying not to make it too wet. Some bridles can be put into the washing machine for thorough cleaning.

24. To fit the cavesson noseband, position it the width of two fingers below the projecting cheek bone. Then adjust it so that you can fit two fingers between the horse's nose and the noseband.

25. Saddle pads and numnahs should be lifted up into the central gullet of the saddle, before girthing up. This helps to make sure that no pressure is put on the horse's spine.

26. If you do not have the time to give your tack a thorough clean, then it is essential that you clean the bit, brush or wipe clean the girth and brush clean any saddle pad or numnah used. Tack that has not had this basic clean up after use may well cause injury to the horse the next time it is used.

27. The most common injuries caused by an ill-fitting saddle are sores, due to the horse's withers being rubbed and bruised. The horse's back, too, will suffer from bruising, lumps, sores, and pain, all of which could lead to behavioural problems.

28. The most common injury caused by an ill-fitting bridle is a cut mouth. This injury gives the horse a great deal of discomfort; so much so that often it is necessary to rest the horse or use a bitless bridle. Sore areas on the horse's face may also necessitate resting the horse until they have healed. The way to avoid these problems is, of course, to remove the cause.

29. The parts of tack which wear and break most frequently are the stirrup leathers, the girth straps, and the reins (especially rubber-covered reins).

30. The tree, the structure in the middle of the saddle on which it is built, can be broken or twisted quite easily. If a saddle is dropped, and a broken tree results, then that saddle can no

longer be used. To do so would give the horse a severe back injury. The tree can also become twisted if the saddle is carried or stored badly.

31. This is a saddle tree. It is the structure around which the saddle is built.

32. When a rider has dismounted, the stirrups should be run up and secured. Stirrups left dangling can knock against the horse's side and elbows. This could both frighten and injure the horse. Also, stirrup irons can catch on doors and other projections, again causing fright and possible injury.

33. Saddles left on stable doors can easily be knocked off. This will inevitably cause damage. Also, the stable door itself can damage the underside of the saddle.

34. When removing the saddle always lift it away from the horse, don't just drag it off the horse's back. When putting the saddle on, put it in place gently, don't just throw it on. Take care to let the girth down carefully, rather than just dropping it down. The horse's spine and back muscles can easily be damaged if care is not taken when putting on and taking off a saddle. The horse's legs can be bruised and damaged if the girth is not handled carefully.

35. Once a horse has been tacked up, hold it or leave it tied up if you need to go and do something else. If left loose, the horse may get down and roll, thereby damaging both itself and the saddle. Or, the horse may rub its saddle against the wall of the stable and get its bridle or bit hooked up or caught up in its reins.

36. The throatlatch should prevent the bridle from being pulled off over the horse's head. You should be able to fit the width of the your hand between the throatlatch and the horse's cheek.

37. The head is obviously a vulnerable and sensitive part of the horse. Make all movements slow and gentle when putting on or taking off the bridle. Be careful not to crush and bend the ears when putting the bridle over the horse's head. Make sure the bridle does not catch over the horse's eyes and take care not to bruise the inside of the horse's mouth by being careless with the bit.

38. To secure the reins, twist them together. Then thread the throatlatch through the twist and buckle it up. The reins can also be hooked behind the stirrup irons if they are particularly long.

Chapter 3: **Shoeing**

1. A. Coronet band. B. Wall. C. Toe. D. Quarter. E. Periople. F. Heel.
   G. Bulbs of heels. H. Cleft of frog. I. Seat of corn. J. Bars. K. Frog.
   L. Sole. M. White line. N. Wall.
2. The clenches are the ends of the nails. The nails have been driven
   into the horse's foot, to secure the shoe, then knocked over to
   form the clenches. The clenches can be seen on the outside of the
   horse's hoof wall approximately 1 1/2 in (38 mm) from the
   ground surface.
3. After a period of time, as the foot grows longer and the shoe
   begins to work loose, the clenches begin to stick up a little
   instead of being flush with the wall of the hoof. They are then
   referred to as risen clenches.
4. Four indicators that show a horse needs to be re-shod: risen
   clenches; the hoof has started to grow over the shoe; the shoe is
   loose; the hoof has started to break up.
5. A tripod.
6. Horses are generally re-shod every six to eight weeks.
7. Those horses required to do a lot of roadwork may need to be
   shod more often; maybe every four weeks. Some horses' hooves
   would appear to grow more rapidly than others, and some have
   weak feet that need more frequent attention. Any horse which
   does a lot of work will need more frequent visits from the farrier.
8. The horse's hooves are constantly growing, and need to be cut
   back at regular intervals. The hooves will start to grow over the
   shoes, and at this point are referred to as overgrown.
9. If the feet are not cut back as soon as they get a little bit long, the
   horse's balance is affected and lameness and injury can result.
10. The shoes need to be in good condition for road riding. Roads
    can be very slippery, and worn shoes will not give the horse a
    good grip, possibly resulting in falls and serious injury.

Chapter 4: **Routine Daily Tasks**

1. If a vet or interested party request that a horse be stood up for
   them to look at, you should try to make the horse stand square

with its weight evenly distributed over all four feet. In this way the horse's true form and condition can be assessed. If the horse stands awkwardly with a leg or legs trailing, it may give the impression that it has something wrong with it.

2. Always use a bridle. This will give you maximum control of the horse when following the vet's requests. Horses are usually unsettled by the vet's presence and may become jumpy as a result. By using a bridle you should be able to maintain control more safely.

3. When leading a horse in hand, always try to walk level with the horse's shoulder, and hold the horse with one hand close to its chin and the other hand holding the end of the reins or rope. In this way you should have good control and be able to observe the horse's reactions.

4. To trot up a horse you should be equipped with gloves, strong footwear and possibly a hard hat; the horse should be wearing a bridle. Keep the horse straight and on a firm level surface. Trot it actively away from the observer, slow to a walk, and turn the horse around carefully. When the horse is straight and balanced again, trot it actively back towards the observer.

5. The handler is using a bridle for good control and is wearing a hard hat, gloves and strong footwear for her own protection. She has positioned herself level with the horse's shoulder so that the horse walks with her and does not drag along behind.

6. Using a bridle gives you more control. If the horse becomes excited and strong, you should be able to regain control if a bridle is used; but, if you are using a headcollar, you may lose control of the horse.

7. A haynet is potentially dangerous to the horse. If the horse should get its legs caught in the haynet a serious accident could follow. By tying up the haynet correctly you minimise the risk of accidents.

8. When lifting a heavy item, it is essential always to keep your back straight and knees bent. Be well balanced, to avoid injury.

9. She should use her leg muscles to push up, rather than her back muscles to drag the item.

10. Take care to lead a horse straight so that it enters through the centre of a stable doorway. Do not try to turn it until you are clear

of the doorway. If you turn the horse before it is clear of the doorway, it may catch its side or hips on the hard edges. This may cause a serious injury.

11. Safe clothing includes gloves, strong footwear (preferably with steel toecaps) and a hard hat.

12. When holding a horse for the farrier or a vet, stand at the horse's head, slightly to one side. Keep on the same side of the horse as the farrier or vet. In this way you can bring the horse's head towards you, so that its hindquarters swing away from you, and the other person if necessary. Also, by standing slightly to one side you avoid being struck into if the horse should strike out with a foreleg.

13. When carrying buckets of water, it is best to take two buckets at once, one in each hand, so you remain balanced and do not twist or lean. Again, always keep your back straight.

Chapter 5: **Bedding and Mucking Out**

1. Straw, shavings, Aubiose, and paper, are all types of bedding in common use.

2. A four-pronged fork, a wheelbarrow, shovel and broom are good tools to use for mucking out a straw bed.

3. A shavings fork, broom, shovel, wheelbarrow, skip and rubber gloves are useful for mucking out a shavings bed.

4. The worker is using a four-pronged fork to remove droppings from a straw bed. Then she is placing the droppings into a wheelbarrow.

5. If the horse's bed is just skipped out daily, leaving the main part of the bed undisturbed, it is called deep litter. The droppings and wet patches are removed. The bedding is topped up. The main part of the bed is not disturbed.

6. To completely muck out a straw bed, first remove all the obvious piles of droppings with the fork. Then work through the whole bed, forking the soiled bedding into the wheelbarrow and the clean bedding into a clean corner of the stable. Sweep the floor clean. Replace the clean bedding and top up as necessary.

7. Stable tools are potentially dangerous. If left untidily around the yard they could cause injury to horse and human. To prevent

accidents keep tools in a designated area.

8. To completely muck out a shavings bed, first remove any obvious piles of droppings with the shavings fork or use the rubber gloves. Then work through the whole bed with the shavings fork or the rubber gloves, putting the soiled bedding into the skip or the wheelbarrow, and move the clean bedding into one area. Sweep the floor clean then put the bedding back down and top up as necessary.

9. Horses are always likely to fidget and move around. By keeping the horse tied up while you are mucking out you can partly restrict its movement and help to make sure that it does not walk into the wheelbarrow or other stable tools, which may cause injury.

10. The fork illustrated is a shavings fork. The other items of stable equipment are: a wheelbarrow used for taking soiled bedding to the muck heap – and often used for moving heavy items around the stable yard; and a skip and rake which are useful for the removal of droppings from the horse's bed when skipping up during the day.

11. When mucking out you are moving dirty bedding around the stable. If the water bucket is left in the stable, some of the dirty bedding is certain to fall into the water. To keep the water clean, remove the bucket from the stable before you begin mucking out.

12. It would be easy for the horse to get caught up on the handles of a wheelbarrow if they are protruding into the stable. Therefore, it is best to place the wheelbarrow across the doorway, so it is accessible but the handles are pointing away from the horse.

13. Wheelbarrows are quite large items and have many protrusions. As they are mobile and often used for carrying heavy items, not just used for mucking out, it is likely that they may be left in all different areas of the yard at all different times. Consequently, both horse and human may find a wheelbarrow in their way at some time. Therefore, always put wheelbarrows away in a safe designated area as soon as you have finished using them.

14. "Skipping up" (sometimes called "skipping out") is the term used for removing droppings from the horse's bedding or any other area, at any time.

15. This is a straw bed. For skipping up, a four-pronged fork or

rubber gloves and a skip would be needed.

16. This is a shavings bed. For skipping up, a shavings fork or rubber gloves and a skip would be needed.

17. It is best to skip up continuously while working on the yard. Otherwise, aim to skip up about three to four times a day.

18. If the horse's feet are picked out into a skip it keeps the yard or stable area clean and saves you from having to sweep and shovel up the debris.

19. By skipping up at regular intervals you keep the yard and the horses' bedding clean. This saves work and helps to preserve the bedding.

20. A stable fork can obviously cause an injury if a horse was to swing into it while it was being used for skipping up. By using rubber gloves you avoid that risk.

21. Muck heaps become very hot, and can spontaneously combust. Being made up of flammable materials it doesn't take long for them to catch fire.

22. If possible, the muck heap should be sited in an easily accessible area. Yard workers need to be able to get to the muck heap easily to save time and energy, and tractors or lorries need good access so they can remove the muck heap from time to time. As there is always a risk of fire or disease with the muck heap, it should be sited well away from buildings.

23. Muck heaps are a potential fire hazard and should be controlled. If left to sprawl across the yard the risk of spreading fire is much greater. The muck heap can also be a place where rats and mice may gather, so it is important to keep this hazard under control too.

24. If the yard is kept tidy it helps to minimise the risk of disease and accidents and the risk of fire. Dirty yards littered with hay and straw help a fire to spread should there be one. Yards littered with tools and other items are hazardous to animal and human.

25. "Setting fair" is the term used for giving the yard a final tidy and check. For example, before going to lunch, or going home, or locking up at night. You skip up the stables, check that all items of equipment have been put away, make sure stable bolts are secure and so on.

Chapter 6: **Points of the Horse, Colours and Markings**

1. A. Poll. B. Withers. C. Loins. D. Point of hip. E. Gaskin. F. Hock. G. Fetlock. H. Tendons. I. Forearm. J. Jugular groove. K. Chin groove. L. Projecting cheek bone.
2. A. Star. B. Stripe. C. White face. D. Blaze. E. Snip. F. White sock. G. White stocking. H. White coronet. I. Ermine marks.
3. Horses have four pasterns, one on each leg.
4. An ergot is a small horny projection found at the back of the horse's fetlock joint.
5. Horses have four chestnuts, one on each leg. Chestnuts are small horny lumps, with an approximate circumference about the size of a 50 pence piece, and can grow to a length of some 2–3 in (50–76 mm) before they break off naturally. They have no purpose and, like the ergot, chestnuts are the residual remains of the early species from which horses are descended, which once had toes.
6. The dock is the bony section which runs from the top of the horse's hindquarters, being the end of the spine and from which the tail hair grows.
7. Knowing the name of each of the points of the horse makes for easier communication. For example, when explaining to a vet where a horse has a wound, or a rash, or some other problem.
8. A sock is a white leg stretching from the hoof any distance up towards the knee or hock. A stocking is a white leg stretching from the hoof, up and over the knee or hock.
9. A bay horse has a brown-coloured coat and black mane and tail. Bays often have black points.
10. A chestnut horse is yellow-brown and has a mane and tail of similar colouring to the rest of its body.
11. A dorsal or eel strip is a black stripe running the length of the horse's spine, from its withers to the top of its tail.
12. A snip is a small white marking on or near the nostrils of a horse.
13. Palomino.
14. Skewbald.
15. A dark bay.
16. A blaze is a broad white stripe down the front of the horse's face.
17. A star is a small white marking in the middle of the horse's forehead.

18. A horse with brown and white patches is called a skewbald.
19. A horse with black and white patches is called a piebald.
20. The person pictured is measuring the height of the horse using a measuring stick.
21. Grey horses may be described as iron-grey, dappled-grey, or flea-bitten grey.
22. Roans can be described as strawberry roan, blue roan, and bay roan.
23. Ermine marks are small black marks on a horse's white sock.

Chapter 7: **Horse Behaviour**

1. Normal horse behaviour, when horses are out together in the field, is relaxed and grazing. Individual horses may be together in ones and twos, but otherwise fairly spread out. Some may be standing at rest and others may be lying down.
2. On a cold wet day you may see the horses huddled together with their tails to the wind, heads down, trying to protect each other from the weather. On a hot sunny day you may see horses seeking shade under the trees. Or they may stand head to tail with their companions; this enables the group to swish flies away from each other's faces.
3. It is instinctive in the horse: to take flight if frightened; to follow the herd; and to protect its offspring.
4. When confined in a stable, a frightened horse is likely to rush around in circles and rush to and from the back of the stable to the doorway.
5. If frightened, horses in a group may take flight together, forming a closer herd as they do so. Having then travelled a short distance, they might stop and turn to survey what had caused the fright.
6. A frightened horse will shy away from the object of its fright, and any other horses with it are likely to shy away at the same time.
7. Anything out of the ordinary, that is new to the horse, may frighten it. Dustbins, plastic bags, litter that flaps and moves in the wind, can also be frightening. Humans and other animals that appear suddenly – for example, a dog rushing out, a human appearing from behind a hedge, or a cyclist suddenly coming by – can all be frightening.

8. Splitting up a group of horses is likely to cause problems. The herd instinct causes horses to want to stay together. If separated, any of them may become worried and excited and try to rush back to the other group.

9. As novice riders are less experienced in coping with the horse's different reactions, it is important to choose a horse that is placid in temperament. Placid horses are less likely to behave unpredictably, and are usually of a steady nature, so less likely to cause an accident.

10. These horses appear to be play fighting.

11. These horses are displaying aggressive behaviour. They have their ears pinned back and it is quite apparent that they are not happy with each other.

12. A "fresh" horse is one that has not had much exercise recently and as a result is full of energy and keen to work off some of that energy. It is likely to be in a hurry to get going, jogging and maybe trying to buck.

13. When riding in company be aware of the reactions of other horses. If a horse puts its ears back, and swings its head towards another horse, maybe threatening to bite at the same time, it is showing its displeasure. If a horse begins swishing its tail and then moves its hindquarters towards another horse, that is another way of showing that it is unhappy with the other horse coming near.

14. One horse out in a field, standing detached from the rest of the group, perhaps with its head down, may be a sign something is wrong. If a horse is lying flat out in the field on a wet or cold day, this is also a cause for concern. A horse which appears to have been in one place, without moving, for a long time, would require investigation.

15. A horse left alone in the field would be looking for the rest of the herd and is likely to canter around, calling for its friends. The horse may run up and down the fence and to and from the gate and may even try to jump out. This behaviour can be traced to the strong herding instinct of horses.

16. Horses are creatures of habit. Through routine they learn how to behave in different situations and what to expect. Changes in routine unsettle them and make them feel insecure.

17. Some likely routines are: the daily feeding times; mucking out and riding times; and the order in which daily yard duties take place.

18. Some horses are particularly boisterous, and may play-fight and canter around in the field more than others. This can lead to injury. In some cases a particularly timid horse might find itself cornered by a more dominant horse and this too can lead to injury. Mares and geldings may fight in the field, during the spring and when the mares start to come into season.

19. A new horse in the field is anxious to explore its surroundings. At the same time, the other horses in the field will want to meet the new horse. This generally results in trotting and cantering around, and some kicking and squealing, until they have all found out about each other.

20. Horses stabled for a long period will be very keen to be let loose in a field and have their freedom. When released they are likely to canter off and buck and kick.

21. Any horse should feel safe in its stable. There should be plenty of room for free movement. It helps if the horse can see other horses and also what is going on in its immediate area. There should be a yard rule that everyone tries to work quietly and calmly so as not to disturb and unsettle the horses.

22. If you approach a stabled horse and it immediately puts its ears back, or retreats to the back of its stable, or turns its hindquarters towards you, be cautious. These are all signs that the horse may be difficult to handle.

23. If stables are open plan – as in the "American Barn" system – horses can see people approaching and will not be startled. If housed in a more conventional stable with just a top door to look out through, a horse may not hear or see you approaching until the last moment. This may startle the horse. If you talk as you approach the stable, the horse will have plenty of warning and should remain calm.

24. First, you should encourage the horse to come to the stable door, so you can go in and put on its headcollar immediately. Then make sure that the horse is securely tied up at all times. Move around the horse carefully, and avoid passing behind its hindquarters. Go under its neck to change sides.

25. Horses have good peripheral vision, but they also have blind spots. If a horse's head is not turned in the direction of its handler the horse may not realise that it is about to be touched. The sudden touch will then startle it and maybe cause a kick or panic reaction. So, always make sure that the horse can see you as you approach. Place a hand on the horse's shoulder then keep contact with the horse as you move to other areas of its body. In this way, through feel, the horse always knows where you are and will not be startled.

26. Some horses do lie down in their stables a great deal. This is actually a good sign because only a relaxed horse that feels safe would do so. Once you get to know an individual horse you will come to know if lying down is normal for that horse, or a cause of concern.

27. Horses like routine. Once familiar with your routines, they are more relaxed because they know what to expect and when. A sudden change in routine may confuse and unsettle them.

28. Open plan stabling, in which the horses can see out all around them, helps to give each horse a feeling of security, as it is maintaining its herd status. Horses gain confidence from having the company of other horses and should therefore be settled and relaxed.

Chapter 8: **The Horse's Health**

1. Clear eyes. Clean nostrils. A shiny coat. Normal behaviour patterns. Well furnished body. Passing normal droppings. Elastic skin, which reacts well to the skin pinch test. Salmon pink mucous membranes. These are all signs of good health in the horse.

2. Discharge from eyes and nose. Dull, starey coat. Inelastic skin. Excessively fat or very underweight. Discoloured mucous membranes. A depressed demeanour and abnormal behaviour.

3. A bright alert expression. Standing squarely on all four feet. Body well furnished. A shining coat.

4. The horse's coat is a reflection of its general health and well-being. If shiny and smooth it is a good sign. If the coat is dull, and rough, it is a bad sign.

5. Normal droppings should be well formed and break on hitting the ground. If the droppings are very loose, or very hard, it is an indication that there is some sort of digestive upset, or a more complicated problem.

6. There may be lumps, growths, or lesions on the horse's skin, which cannot be seen. By running a hand over the horse you can feel for these problems. You can also locate areas of abnormal heat, which can be a sign of injury or illness developing.

7. If your horse is normally an alert animal and interested in its surroundings, you should be concerned if its behaviour appears dull and lethargic.

8. A "staring coat" appears dull and tends not to lie flat giving the appearance that the horse may be a little cold.

9. The horse is going to be left unobserved for a long period through the night, whether field-kept or stabled. The last check you make is to ensure that everything is as safe and in order as possible. For example, are the rugs really secure, is there plenty of water for the horse, is there food available, and so on? The following morning your first check is to make sure nothing untoward has happened through that long period when the horse was not under observation.

10. Last thing at night, check the horse has plenty of clean water, and has enough food. Rugs, if worn, must be well adjusted. The field or stable must be completely secure. Check that there is nothing left in the stable or field that may cause injury. Finally, make sure that your horse appears in normal good health.

11. First thing in the morning check that your horse greets you in its customary manner. Make sure rugs are adjusted. Check and top up water as necessary. Observe the stable or field and check that there is nothing unusual in it and that no damage has occurred during the night.

12. In this type of stabling, the horses can all see each other. This helps to create the feeling of being together as a herd.

13. By reporting your worries about a horse's health immediately, however small, you may prevent a serious problem. The horse may have the beginnings of an ailment, which could turn into something serious, but if treated straight away, is only minor.

14. Any abnormal behaviour, such as lying down a lot, rolling, look-

ing at flanks, appearing depressed, holding up a leg, are all signs that the horse may benefit from a vet's attention.

Chapter 9: **Care of the Horse and the Horse's Field**

1. Check there is no debris in the field. Make sure the water supply is plentiful and functioning normally. Observe trees and plants and ensure there are no poisonous ones. Make sure all gates and fencing are secure and not in need of repair.
2. By making these daily checks you will help to promote a safe and healthy environment for your horse, and therefore help to prevent injury and disease.
3. Field-kept horses should be provided with water, shelter, good grazing and company.
4. If the droppings are removed from the field daily it will help to prevent the spread of worms and ensure more healthy grass growth. Also, pull up and remove weeds and any poisonous plants.
5. As can be seen in the illustration, "pig wire" can be dangerous as horses can get their feet stuck in the squares. Barbed wire will cause injury if horses try to lean over it and it can tear rugs worn by horses.
6. If a field is over grazed, the grazing will become poor. Horses should be moved on to fresh pasture from time to time, to give each field a chance for a period of re-growth.
7. The term "horse sick" describes a field which has been over grazed, leaving bare and poached areas. There will be an excess of droppings and weeds in abundance. And there may be some poisonous plants.
8. The horses should be removed from the field. The droppings should be collected, and steps taken to eradicate the weeds. The field should then be harrowed and rested, with possibly some fertiliser applied. It should not be grazed again until there is a good re-growth of grass.
9. When turning out a horse, lead it to the field using a headcollar and rope. Open the gate wide to give the horse plenty of room to walk into the field. Turn the horse back towards the gate and

close the gate securely. Then slip off the headcollar. If there is more than one horse, all the horses should have their headcollars removed at the same time. Do not chase the horses away, let them move away quietly and make sure you keep clear of their hindquarters.

10. Take a headcollar and rope and maybe a small titbit in your pocket. Encourage the horse to come to the gate to greet you. Slip on the headcollar and then give the titbit.

11. Horses that are difficult to catch may surrender more easily if all the other horses in the field are removed first. Approach the horse, if it will not come to you, with the headcollar concealed behind your back. Offer a titbit. Be patient and gain the horse's confidence before trying to put the headcollar on.

12. When bringing horses out of the field, take care to give them plenty of room in the gateway, but make sure loose horses do not escape. Make sure also that the gate is closed securely behind you.

13. A bucket of feed is usually like a magnet to all horses. If a group of horses is in the field and you take a bucket in, the horses will all gather hoping for a feed and soon fighting, kicking and biting will begin. Apart from possibly injuring each other, the horses are quite likely to injure you.

14. Horses wearing turnout rugs must be checked frequently. Rugs tend to slip easily and can break if horses are playing in the field. Once slipped or broken, the rug becomes a hazard to the horse. Keep a regular check on rugs.

15. In the summer horses must have adequate shade from the sun. They may also need respite from flies which can make horses miserable. Check on your horses at regular intervals each day, to make sure they are not being bothered unduly. If particularly stressed, the horses may end up trotting around the field continuously, trying to get some relief from the flies.

16. This post and rail will provide strong, secure fencing. The bottom rail prevents horses from escaping underneath the fence; and fixing the rails on the inside of the fence posts stops them being pushed loose.

17. If a field becomes particularly waterlogged and muddy during the winter, horses may suffer from a number of ailments on their

lower limbs and have problems with their feet. In very wet weather, some horses not wearing rugs may also be prone to a variety of skin diseases.

18. The water trough can supply two fields at once. Also, positioned in this way, it prevents horses becoming trapped behind it.

Chapter 10: **Feeding and Watering**

1. (a) Feed little and often. Horses are trickle feeders and they have only small stomachs. (b) Feed plenty of bulk. The horse's digestive system has evolved to function best digesting larger amounts of fibre than concentrate feed. (c) Do not make any sudden changes to the diet; the horse has a population of bacteria in its gut, which help to digest feed. These bacteria are quite specific to different feeds and sudden changes will cause an imbalance in the population of bacteria and therefore feed may not be properly digested. (d) Allow one to one-and-a-half hours after feeding before exercising. The horse's stomach lies close to the lungs and a full stomach may restrict the function of the lungs. Horses need time to digest a feed before beginning exercise. (e) Use only clean receptacles and good quality feed. Dirty feed bowls are likely to discourage horses from eating and they may harbour disease. Poor quality feed can lead to poor digestion and unthriftiness.

2. (a) Water before feeding, to make sure the horse does not feel the need to take a long drink after feeding, which may cause the feed to be washed too rapidly through the system, and the digestive juices to be diluted. (b) A plentiful supply of water should always be available. Approximately 70 per cent of the horse is water, and water is needed for all bodily functions. (c) Keep the water supply clean. The water in stables will absorb ammonia which will make the water unpleasant for the horse, and in the field debris may drop into the water, again making it unpleasant for the horse to drink.

3. Horse and pony nuts should be clean and dry. They should smell fresh and not crumble.

4. If there is any sign of mould, or if nuts smell mouldy, or if they

crumble and appear damp, then consider them to be inferior.

5. Rolled oats should be of a pale yellow colour. They should smell fresh. There should be an equal ratio of kernel to husk.

6. If the oats are grey in colour, or if they smell mouldy, or there seems to be more husk than kernel, then consider them inferior in quality.

7. Shredded sugar beet should be dark grey in colour. The shreds should be dry and firm and sweet smelling.

8. If the sugar beet has a green tinge to its colour, or if it smells mouldy, or is damp, consider it inferior in quality.

9. Coarse mix should have a variety of different grains and other items in the mix. It should smell fresh and be fairly moist. All the grains should be of a good colour.

10. If the coarse mix is stuck together, in lumps, or smells mouldy, or seems to have only one type of grain, then consider it of poor quality.

11. Bran should be a pale pink colour, with white flecks. It should be dry and the flakes separate and loose. It should smell fresh and, if you put your hand well into a bag which is full of bran, your hand should come out with a white floury covering.

12. If the bran is stuck together in clumps, or smells of mould and has no flour dust in it, then consider it of poor quality.

13. The oats grain has a separate outer husk, which breaks away from the kernel. Oats tend to be slimmer than barley grains. Barley grains are more plump and have an outer husk which remains attached to the grain.

14. Molassed chaff is fairly dark brown in colour with some strands of yellow straw. It should smell sweet and be quite moist and open in texture.

15. If the molassed chaff smells mouldy, or is dusty, or if it is stuck together in clumps, then consider it of inferior quality.

16. Meadow hay should contain a variety of different grasses. There should be no weed. It should smell sweet and be a pale green colour, or a pale yellow.

17. If weeds are present in the meadow hay, or if it smells mouldy, or if it is grey-brown in colour, then consider it of poor quality.

18. Poor quality feeds are often dusty and mouldy. This dust and mould can lead to respiratory problems, sometimes colic, and

general unthriftiness.

19. "Hard" feed is the term used to encompass the grain feed and other manufactured feed, such as pony nuts, given to horses.

20. The 14.2 hh pony would probably do well fed on pony nuts, with perhaps some sugar beet. A small amount of molassed chaff could be given, or maybe a very low-energy coarse mix.

21. Three small feeds a day are better for the pony than one or two larger ones. Probably only 1–1 1/2 lb (454–680 g) in each feed is needed.

22. If the pony was not inclined to get overweight, it could have an unlimited supply of hay. but where it is necessary to control the amount fed, to prevent the pony from becoming overweight, 5–6 lb (2.25–2.72 kg) morning, lunch and evening would be a good ration.

23. The pony could have the same types of feed but be given more.

24. Three feeds a day would be best, and the pony could have approximately 3 lb (1.3 kg) in each feed.

25. The pony should have an unlimited supply of hay.

26. The 15.3 hh horse could have a low-energy coarse mix or, if the owner preferred, a mixture of sugar beet, rolled barley, and chaff, either molassed or plain.

27. Three feeds a day would be best. Each feed could have a total of 3 lb (1.3 kg) of hard feed.

28. Approximately 16 lb (7.25 kg) of meadow hay per day, divided into three feed times.

29. The horse could have the same types of feed, just a little more quantity.

30. A good ration would be 4 lb (1.8 kg) of hard feed in each feed, three times a day.

31. Provided that the horse is not inclined to be overweight, it should be given an unlimited supply of hay.

Chapter 11: **General Knowledge**

1. There are many reflective and fluorescent items, which can be worn by horse and human for road riding. Hat covers, jackets

and coats, are the most popular for riders. The horse can be equipped with an exercise sheet, a tail cover, boots or leg bands, all made of fluorescent materials.

2. Verges have many, hidden, dangers. There could be bottles, cans, and other debris, some not immediately visible. Also, if a horse should shy at something and step off the verge on to the road, passing traffic may be taken by surprise and an accident could result. For these reasons it is best to remain on the road, where traffic will allow extra room to pass the ride, and just use the verge as an emergency area to move on to if in difficulty.

3. When crossing roads, the whole ride should always stay together. If the horses are divided up, there is a risk of some horses trying to follow the others, possibly causing them to step out into the path of traffic.

4. A fluorescent exercise sheet and fluorescent leg bands would aid visibility.

5. Roads are often very slippery. Knee boots will protect horses' knees if they slip or stumble and fall.

6. Keep a lookout for anything that may cause your horse to shy out into the traffic. For example, a loose dog, a person coming out of their house or working in their garden, a dustbin partially obscured, flapping debris on the roadside, and so on.

7. If a road is quiet and its surface not slippery then the ride will be safe enough to trot in straight lines, but never around bends. Trot steadily, never fast, to prevent damage to the horse's legs.

8. When leading along a road, the horse should have a bridle on and the handler should have gloves and clothing that are easy to see. These precautions will make both horse and handler clearly visible to oncoming traffic.

9. When leading keep to the right hand side of the road, as pedestrians should. The handler should be positioned between the horse and the traffic.

10. Four rules a ride should observe: (a) keep to bridleways and other areas where you have been given permission to ride and do not ride on private land; (b) always leave gates as you find them, unless one has obviously been left open by mistake, allowing livestock to roam; (c) ride around the edges of fields, never across the crop; and (d) be courteous to any other countryside users.

11. Always tell someone where you intend to go on your ride and approximately how long you intend to be out. This person can then seek help if you do not return, or if your horse returns without you.

12. If you meet others, always slow to a walk, and make sure they are aware of your presence. Do not ride too close to pedestrians or other riders.

13. If the road is quite wide and straight, it can be helpful to ride two abreast. In this way you make yourselves more visible, and encourage drivers to make a more careful effort to pass you.

14. A well-schooled horse can be kept under control better than one that is not well schooled. You should be more able to cope with the horse shying, or taking a dislike to an object if it is schooled.

15. If a person falls off on the road, and the horse runs loose, make sure the person is attended to first then inform someone who will be able to help and look for the horse as soon as possible. If there are enough helpers it would be a good idea to position a person, with highly visible clothing, at a strategic point to warn drivers that they may meet a loose horse in the road.

16. If a person is unconscious, you should check their airway is clear. Speak to them as much as possible, as this may help to bring them around, and will reassure them. Loosen tight clothing, and stem any obvious bleeding. Do not try to move them unless they are in danger of choking, in which case they should be put in the recovery position.

17. Anyone who has hit their head may suffer from concussion. If they remount, and later have a dizzy spell or black out, they are in danger of falling off again. To prevent further injury and accident, the person should walk home on foot.

18. A fire notice should have the following printed on it: In the Event of Fire, Raise the Alarm. Move Horses to Safety. Dial 999 For the Fire Brigade. Fight the Fire.

19. Keep the yard areas tidy. Keep the muck heap tidy and away from buildings. Have a no smoking policy throughout the yard.

20. There should be a number of fire extinguishers distributed around the yard. Full water troughs and hoses attached to taps will be of great help. Buckets should be available to carry both sand and water. All these items can help in the event of fire.

21. The British Horse Society aims to improve the general standard of horse and pony welfare in Great Britain. To improve awareness of the horse generally. To improve the standard of equitation and horse knowledge amongst all sections of the riding and carriage driving public. To provide benefits for Society members. To improve access to the countryside for the riding and driving public.